# SOMETHING ABOUT

POETRY BY
ANDRENA ZAWINSKI

BLUE LIGHT PRESS ◆ 1ST WORLD PUBLISHING

1ˢᵗ WORLD
PUBLISHING

SAN FRANCISCO ◆ FAIRFIELD ◆ DELHI

## Something About

## 1st World Publishing
106 South Court Street
Fairfield, Iowa 52556
www.1stworldpublishing.com

## Blue Light Press
1563 45th Avenue
San Francisco, California 94122

## Cover and Book Design
Melanie Gendron
www.melaniegendron.com

## Cover Art
"Ophelia in the Lotus Garden (who is yet to appear . . .)"
38" x 24" oil on panel
Copyright ©2009 by Jane Hyland
hylandj@carnegiemnh.org

## First Edition

LCCN: 2009938224

ISBN: 978-1-4218-9136-1

# Table of Contents

## 1.

## 2.

## 3.

# 4.

# 5.

# 1.

*In the very essence of poetry there is something indecent:*
*a thing is brought forth which we didn't know we had in us*
*so we blink our eyes, as if a tiger had sprung out*
*and stood in the light, lashing its tail . . .*

—Czeslaw Milosz

# THE POET DRIVING

The poet,
white knuckled
at the podium, drives
the crowd. And reeling,
as if taking on mountainous S curves,
or hydroplaning minefields,
the poet maps metaphors
in shag bark and hickory, staggering
the dappled sundown.

This could be
Kansas, Saigon, Mozambique, Peoria,
a road, bridge, underpass
where the poet dresses deathbeds
in thin sheets of memory.
The clenched fist
becomes an open hand,
fingers that point
press into prayer.

And our silences
grow ravenous for this.
We choke down whole landscapes,
drink in cloud bursts, throb
with the starlit sky. We lean into the words
like a slow dance pinned to ourselves
like a corsage, like a lover, like a poem,
like the language
of applause.

# Writing Lesson

You knew you were in trouble
the second you put the plate on the table—
those sesame snow peas and truffles
you drizzled with kumquat and ginger
to impress your poetry potluck writing group—
when he said, *Not Chinese again.*

You knew you were in-for-it
when he called your poem a travelogue of Paris
grinding down the wrong track
with its Kunitz epigraph fumbling at the gears
as he blasted, *The old man got to wear*
*that crown of Laureate just for his age.*

You knew, despite your mince and trim
and folding in its metaphoric light,
this poem would be tied to the chair
with rope, have the life beaten from it,
a flabby bunch of bunkum flattened
with his belting, *Where is the cri de coeur?*

And you knew in the way you know
in a half-wake state when you hear a train
in the distance barreling into your sleep
in a blur of whistles and grinds and whirs,
its metal scraping rails in a still night, deep
in dark, its muffled blue note wailing.

You knew you must be dreaming this
standing before a train coming on headlong
at you half-naked there, a train about to slice
through what you peeled down to—
an awful tutu, mismatched shoes, feather cloche
you shouldn't be caught dead in.

Then this man with a train for a mouth
tells you this is not a well-lit poem
and the guy donning laurels in the first car
misdirected it—that it's rocketing
down the wrong track on a collision course
headed right for Gare du Nord.

And you actually thank this man, talking
with a mouthful of train, for his keen observation.
But you don't write a word for days
then weeks as you focus instead your eyes
on wind riding dunes hitched to a slice
of tangerine light, shapeshifting sunset.

You put your ear to the movement of earth
beneath a frenzy of shorebirds pecking the eyes
from a head of a beached seal there. And speechless,
you listen for a fading blue note of a train
in the distance, off to somewhere far away.

# CURIOSITY PIECE

*. . . it is surprising how the morning air gives one ideas!*
—Scenes de la Boheme

Facing the blank of the wall,

turning toward the window, distracted
by a Puccini aria blasting from a *Speedpack* box
at the *Car-O-Van* blocking the sidewalk—
a neighbor is packing up a life, all the odd
whatnots, curious thingamabobs,
those whatchamacallits. No passerby veers
from the bellow of the taped tenor,
from the pell-mell of the sidewalk—each stops,
has to stop, heads ticking back and forth.

Words drift this way and that

in from the fussy street, and I am distracted
as another curiosity piece enters the scene—
a sea blue '52 custom Ford pickup
pulling up to the curb, a woman
in a cracked black leather jacket,
in low slung jeans and velvet high tops,
hair a slick of purple pomade, singing,
singing along in a froggy single-speaker rattle
to *La Boheme*.

Flightless bird beneath a storm-scratched sky,

I try to chip out my own sound
beneath this canvas of noisy spring flyway,
but I am distracted by Our Lady of Lourdes
church bells chiming in almost midday
and something else I am getting up to do
that I forget in an instant, yet something
curiously more important now
than facing the blank of the wall—

where corners web with dust.

# OPEN STAGE

(at the Horse & Cart Café, Charleston SC)

You have walked all day the length of streets,
cataloged anything of importance that has been here
before: Tide at the seawall. The cadence of wind.
Poems moving in. The church bells chime.
A car starts. Some stranger remarks on the brilliance
of sun. Palmettos bow to the weight of air.

You walk until your legs say: *Sit down. Enter
a café.* The day blows in on door hinge reeds.
You eye the sky so bold a blue, a breathy blinding blue,
you think someone will steal off with it, frame it
in the coarse of sailcloth for a windowless wall.
The register chings. A phone rings. Metal scoops ice.

The room lights up. You read over someone's
shoulder a late edition: Same sex couples marry
in San Francisco. A female astronaut on Mir.
Hyakutake in view, stars spill from the gourd
of dream, do what they please. Poets sort sheaves,
track second thought verse in fine point notes.

A man joins you at your table. You have met
this man before in Pittsburgh, Paris, Charleston.
He buys you coffee, wine, brown sugar pie
in exchange for conversation about his stock
acquisitions, the travels seaside, paintings of sky.
The room's dizzy spirit dances with nerve.

Poets on cue cross the stage: A quivering heart
turns over words, delicate as new shoots on spring
bulbs. A waitress at the cash box sorts checks,
counts the stiffs, searches pockets hoping
she can make it up. Breath beads the window
in a blur. Hummingbirds circle feed.

Sweat glistens the brow. Hand a tremble,
an old man's voice cracks like a schoolboy's.
A girl in red, tattooed and pierced, reads fire
between her legs, a passion for learning
as if it's by heart. A man whispers *white trash*,
then relieves himself in a dozen public couplets.

Cadets chuckle the backdrop. You wait for a clearing
in the sound. You think you could inhabit all these
voices all at once, move inside them like a baby
about to be born. You are up to read.
Your eyelid quivers, breath starts. The room takes on
a new night chill. The register rings, door swings.
You see the girl has gone, her scarlet petallike
stain left signing the lip of her cup. The sky,
dark, moans at the glass.

# ALMOST ANYTHING CAN HAPPEN HERE

*Slavery was a bad thing, and freedom, of the kind we got,*
*with nothing to live on, was bad. Two snakes full of poison . . .*
*The snake called slavery lay with his head pointed south,*
*and the snake called freedom lay with his head pointed north.*
—Patsy Mitchner's slave narrative in *My Folks Don't Want Me*
*to Talk About Slavery*

Almost anything can happen here
in this poem. The sky brighten yellow
with morning sun. A snake appear,
cross sandy sweetgrass, coil in viny figs
stirring up the language of insects
and birds. The wind sigh high
in moss hung cyprus.

A girl could arrive, coming to her nature,
barefoot and naked. Playing, singing,
maybe dancing. Others off picking,
spinning, weaving, stitching. The soil
is good. The honey sweet. Money in
from the ships. The wind might rise,
palmettos bow.

Or it is near night. A veil of dusk
on the seawall. Quince flowering
white. Houses quiet as museum pieces.
Grand columns at porticos crested
by crenelated parapets, dressed
in piazzas and cupolas
wrought by indigo hands.

Or there is a log hut with sand floor,
stick and dirt chimney. The girl tills
a patch into moonlight for blue-eyed flax,
long-legged grain. Eats ash cakes and meat
fat as butter. Sleeps on a straw bed
as sky slips in roof slits, bright splinters
of light stretched across rafters.

The streets here are cobbled with voices
of ghosts. On the tongue Gullah slung
in high pitched rifts, low guttural moans.
They are singing, weaving, fingers twisted
about bone spoons coiling row on row.
Or their backs bucked over barrels, skin
striped in swipes of cowhide.

The girl's mother could appear here.
A wet-nurse toting bundles, holding a candled
stance of flowers, pitcher fixed on her head.
Some bow to her who saw her crowned
across the seas. And there is the block
that centers the street for buying
and selling. And the gallows for hanging.

Oh, it must grow dark and rain in this
poem. The girl runs. Bushes slap
her legs in field rows full of rain frogs,
whippoorwills hollering treetops. A rack
of north clouds, dark as crows, rolling up
the main road. A cannon thundering
from a club hole in the sky.

Another snake winds in. Both meet
at her feet. She shakes a bag-of-jack rattling
spells and chants and charms. They move in
closer. The snake called Slavery, his head
pointed South. The snake called Freedom,
his head pointed North. Two snakes strike,
both full of poison.

Night stays on a nocturnal nightjar, a long
lullaby. The girl sleepwalks dunes. Oyster shells
in her palms, held up to the moon, light up
with the language of stars, dream
of sky—everything black
and eternal as Cyprus.

# CALL HER:

Corona for Morning,
Circling Lake Merritt in Oakland, California
and Imagining Paris, France

This morning circling Lake Merritt, the birds
rouse the imagination with squawks, honks,
raspy cries. Slick cormorants line log booms
beating wings at mist, clumsy pelicans
slap at the water's sheen, everything
awake on a snake of lake-light crawling
the gnarl of tree trunks—and Angelina
turns beneath her blanket on dewy grass,
turns there to kiss her lover on his cheek
as they rise there, as he calls out her name
like an urge, like a drive, like a hunger.
So in this poem name him Romero,
because you can. Imagine them instead
as they dance lakeside, Bois de Boulogne.

They dance lakeside at Bois de Boulogne
in Paris, France—dance with the same fluster
as birds circling in a raucous laurel
of wing beats, coos. But this is not Paris
but Oakland, California, and they
are homeless where sentries of city doves
preen at water's edge on the lake wall's lip
along a ducky little waterway.
This could be Bastille Day, could be Paris
dressed in pomp and flair, a firecracker
sky flushed in a blush of hoopla. Lovers
are the thing there. If you are not in love,
you will be, or steal into someone else's,
too much Bordeaux too early in the day.

Too much Bordeaux too early in the day,
name them what you will—him Remy, call her
Adeline, because you can. That's the thing
with poetry, it can pose lovers where
imagination wishes to have them
stir or waken or even dance around
in Paris. Here, part of the scenery
and art of invention, her hand in his
rests for now on her grumbling stomach
while a legion of pigeons guards the bank,
feet a polish of pink, eyes golden sequins,
garden varieties, yet necks lustrous
in a royal sheen of purple and green—
but this poem is not one for the birds.

This poem is not one for the birds, but
it is for that homeless girl blanketed
in this Paris of the imagination
wearing a wide-brimmed hat and scented
lavender, not at this man's coarse and thick
hands grabbing mussels young gulls fuss over,
flurry of feathers caught in the brambles,
city doves strutting their velvet night coats,
pecking peanut shells she scrambles after.
She dances lakeside, Bois de Boulogne,
too much Bordeaux too early in the day
where a sweet rich napoleon calls her
with strong coffee all the muscle she needs,
someone else busy with birds in Oakland.

# Night Watch

(from Kauai, Hawaii)

The cobalt sky is soapy with clouds, and palm fronds bend and sway
above a treasure trove of fish still plying the spiny coral of reef beds.
Tonight, I find my father here, dead thirty years, yet sauntering into
my watch of stars, into lines of a poem I inscribe on a sheet of night.

Later, I will take that dockworker's thumb worn Social Security card,
deposit it in a bank box in California where he once looked for a job.
I'll hold it between my palms, feel it warm in my hands, a bit of sunset
inside the chilly April night he died in Pittsburgh, out of work again.

With it I will place the note he wrote to me in a baby record book,
"I cut your bangs today. You giggled as hairs tickled your nose."
Then the honorable discharge papers from the Air Force,
then the governor's pardon for his penitentiary years.

Next I'll stuff inside his billfold, bulging beneath a rubber band
he wrapped round it so long ago. And all the empty nights he filled
waking me to watch G-men battle gangsters on Swing Shift Theater,
my mother at an assembly line inspecting pans for imperfections.

I'll wedge into the safe box six lit Sparklers one Fourth of July
at Atlantic City, the sticky sweet of salt water taffy on my fingertips,
Bazooka bubblegum fortunes he read to me, the warm musky smell
of his underarm where I nuzzled in as he rocked me to sleep.

I swear to keep them all locked safe inside, never to release them
no matter how clamorous the banging, keep them facts of the matter:
he was forty-seven, gripped by the vise of bum luck and a failed heart.
A shroud of clouds now shape his face, breathy wind a low hum of him.

Hooked to a stranger by genes and geography, I press a milky plumeria,
the graveyard flower and its heady perfume, up against a breast of night,
renew my watch of coastal sky, its dark quiet sulking behind a veil
of illusory lights, all its stormy rings winding round the moon.

11

# STUCK INSIDE

I want to write about a balmy coastal night,
the sky a sweep of clouds, crows diving pines,
feathers of light a gibbous moon flings low,
but I am stuck inside, sipping diner coffee
at a barstool in a Pittsburgh donut shop,
and eavesdropping over the shoulder
of the tenant who occupies my old house,
the place from which my dreams were launched,
and from where she boasts she has hooked up
an extra washer, is taking in laundry, will not pay
the water bills or her rent, and just won't move.

I want to take you with me in this poem
on a sunny walk along the shore, droopy-headed day lilies
dropping blossoms in rows tidy as a run of sailboats
slipping by the San Francisco skyline, neat as kites,
easy and steady on the smooth bay breeze,
a moment's elixir. But back in Pittsburgh,
there are storms driving me into where I watch
my gypsy father, stumble-drunk with wanderlust
and burning with the fire of cognac, staring
from our kitchen window at that frayed clothesline
flagged with bed sheets above a backyard choked
by a flood of dandelions and doldrums.

I want to hold you close to me in this poem
like huckleberry and fern do the mossy trout stream bank,
eucalyptus perfuming air whipping the shoreline highway,
berms puddled in dewy light. But I am crouched inside
a dark corner of somewhere I left behind,
my neighbor's voice rumbling in on the consonant strung tongue
of her Old Country, recounting how she hid with her mother
from soldiers in a grain pipe on some abandoned farm
back when the earth shook and bombs fell
in whistles and booms from above and behind.

I want to wend you with these words
through this shapeshifting landscape past a windbreak
of cypress at the next turn, hand you a nosegay
of seaside daisies blushed pink beside the water's edge.
But back in Pittsburgh, a flurry of noisy night birds
breaks loose again on orthodox church bell peals,
the hillside an echo of women singing a cappella
at the untended grave of my mother, the pinwheel
I propped there for a new year paling in spring light,
blades heavy with the weight of coins I pasted on,
pennies I found tossed in my path by some gods
of good fortune.

Back in Pittsburgh, I get stuck inside, alone
and on my back in bed growing claws and bird wings
to take me where I have come to be, no longer dreaming
windmill farms, their petals spinning celebrants of air
on a palette of sky. But back in Pittsburgh, there is always
this explosion of light in an amusement park where I first met
a mechanical fortune teller queen in a penny arcade,
Esmeralda, who each time I looked for a way out
slid her card predictably down the shoot
with all the words I ever needed:
*good luck, good luck.*

# Intoxicating Morning

(after the Napa Valley Writers' Conference)

The trabajadores lean into the weather beaten fence rail,
casual and easy, near Sunshine Market just off CA 29.
This is wine country where the grapes are bursting
with more intoxicating promise than fields can bare.

The sky flames overhead when my attention turns toward
the *Hola, K'tal* of a man tipping his Giant's cap to me,
melodic as any troubadour. Pruning shears in his hand,
rutty lines tell a fortune of work in the clipping of vines.

But I am too hung over on poetry wandering in and out
of a week's writing retreat and long nights of tasting fiestas
to even acknowledge him with a nod. Maybe if I grew up
in California or Mexico where life sticks close to the sun

I could interpret all the the sounds of this Napa morning,
those stellar jays' early warnings from the mossy oak.
Maybe I could understand the resiliency to work without shade
or fresh water, organoclorines in pesticide spray overhead

as I stumble into the day, tipsy with poetry, turning a deaf ear
to greetings, the Sierra's cabernet still teasing my tongue

# I Am Reminded When Thinking

I am reminded, almost as if in whispers
by weathered house plaques on backstreets
of Prague, that behind the damp and musty
walls, those of some importance once must have

invented themselves above the rest of us here
who, ordinary, press our pens to pads,
our noses to fogged window panes to watch
and clock the melancholic morning drizzle.

Dustbins and brooms push in along the River
Vltava in a hush where shopkeepers drape doors
in lengths of amber beads jostling marionettes,
where sidewalk vendors fling open stall displays,

where I am reminded how shelves are stocked
in a new abundance with buxom breads, aged
cheese, pickled eggs and Postum. But how still now
the boat dock silenced of ragtime bandstands

and jazzy improvisational cafés, how later dim
saloons will dance with consonant strung syllables,
how under doorways, in corridors, behind walls,
some of us will find each other with fingertips and tongues,

how we will make promises and plans, interpret dreams,
float buoyant and rest on the wake of some small slice
of happiness, or on broken speech fill pillows
in relentless streams of muffled grief beneath

rime-colored skies the ravens cry. I am reminded
other mornings will wash in misty above sills,
a flurry of poppies in the rain-cleared air, halos
of canopies shading the light, reminded we are all

but ordinary mortals here taking on these uphill
cobbled paths where Kafka walked and stopped
above the long stretch of red rooftops to watch
how golden the charm of turrets and domes

held captive by this mother with claws,
how we can regret only that we are not birds.

# DRIVING THE LAURELS

(Somerset, PA in the Laurel Mts.)
*. . . all the bright clouds and clusters,*
*beasts and heroes,*
*glittering singers and isolated thinkers*
*at pasture.*
—from Gerald Stern's "Cow Worship"

Driving the Laurels, I wind the regular route to a week of work
before leaving one coast behind for another, Pennsylvania
greening past Somerset. Driving this road where the deer leapt
and fell, legs tucked under, head forest bent, as if to have tried
a last time to lift itself up for one more look back. I drive
these mountains laden with words to fill classrooms I inhabit
in this string of last days east, in my hands these gifts:

Kenyon's peonies and Sandburg's fog, some of Harjo's horses,
one tidy wheelbarrow from Williams. Driving the Laurels past
a store that says *Open* that never is, a roadside sign peddling
gravel and clean fill instead of corn, detour roping an Elks Hall
and Amish draped in black behind bare windows, I drive fast
trying to catch some AM news above the static between hills,
past the silo a funnel cloud lifted last year then dropped down.

I drive fast past willows at the pond's edge, past forsythia
in the patches, Johnny-Jump-Ups nosing through the berm. I work
the week in rural America, cut my way through untamed flowers
to coax from children a long look at what they hold here:
these cows at pasture, their udders fat and heavy with what
we need, and those spring peepers—the high-pitched chorus
they will bring when night rolls down to greet the creek grass.

## Girl with Umbrella

I look up from my local street map,
and there she is. She stops me there,
this little girl dancing in the street.

Dancing, under an arc of rainbow
the garden hose makes, dancing
and skipping in a balancing act
atop her invisible high wire, teetering,
red umbrella turned inside out
and held high above her head,
its dog-eared spokes dripping wildly
with this, this which she was born into,
to be a child, all glee under an arch of water,
ecstatic in the sheer abandon of what children
must be doing all over the world
at fire hydrants wrenched open,
or under downpours of rain,
whole waterfalls upon them,
their eyes squinting and smiling,
steps skittish and impish,
faces tilted upward toward the sun.

And when I stop for her, she looks at me,
then head bent, closes her eyes, backs away,
and in a little curtsy motions me to pass by,
for me to pass through, both of us now
part of the same small moment of poetry.

# 2.

*Art is not about itself but the attention we bring to it.*
—Marcel Duchamp

# SOMETHING ABOUT

(A Winged Sonnet)

Something about these little song sparrows,
their avian tongues and throaty chortles,
the buzzy twittering floundering air
just outside the steamy bedroom window.

Something about the rain, the way it clucks
its testy tongue against the glass a blur
with the setting sun's seductive passion.
Something about these sprightly singers.

Something about the way they tuck themselves
inside their wing bars devoted to feathers.
Something about the heart here pinned inside,
the tick of it, sky so blue, nimbus moon.

Something about this perch beside the pane
to watch day nestle in a moody moonlight.

# DREAMBOAT

(after Magritte's white dress
and thinking of Marilyn Monroe)

So here she comes again,
that big blonde dreamboat
sailing onto the scene,
polished to a sheen,
heady and haloed by seabirds,
sails at her mast billowing
like a finger crooked
and calling you to her.

And you move toward her,
just on the chance
she may ask you to enter
some cabin holding
a geography of mounds
in breasts and buttocks,
and where in the closet hangs
a perfect white dress,

dreaming her body
breathing inside it.

# THE LARGENESS OF FLOWERS

*... So I said to myself, I'll paint what I see, what the flower is to me;
but I'll paint it big, and they will be surprised into taking the time to
look at it.*
—Georgia O'Keeffe

Rising into a day shivering in a rare western gray,
clouds run ragged by wind and rain across the range,
even hottentot sun cups curl in upon themselves
and I become afraid the world might turn to black and white
so I make my way to you, Georgia, inside a gallery garden
filled with the largeness of flowers, a poetry of things.

Like you I love to linger inside the bud and fold of color
upon those petal palettes, whole continents of blooms swelling
in a garden party of the grand. I think as I look in, how can you say
there is no sex in the fiery poppy, no birth in its blood rich petals,
no thought of death inside the deep dark center, no drama
in these big beauties that dizzy and dazzle as any first love might.

You say these flowers mean nothing more than their own largeness,
lines spiraling in upon themselves and taking their natural course.
What starts beneath the soil line appears above the ground
then plucked by you, you bequeathed them to these gallery walls.
On my wall, your wild iris blazes and poppies swell like bodies,
like any love at first sight might in a new found intimacy.

You say none of this means anything, that they are simply flowers
and big. But in the largeness of flowers I can almost see the blood rich
petals of my own mother's lips as my head tunneled past
the spread wren bone, she a sky adrift in twilight clouds like a city
a blur in fog, the sun setting down, unaware of her own pain or of me.
My mother is dead. You are dead. The flowers return.

A garden party of the large, colossal, mammoth, but only flowers
pushing their stubborn heads toward the incessant chatter of birds.

# AGAINST THE WIND

(Pantoum for Angel Island, San Francisco, CA)
*If you come to a land with no ancestors*
*to bless you, you have to be your own*
*ancestor . . .*
—from Shirley Lim's "Riding into California"

A Chinese couple charts family landings at the map, passes time,
as the Angel Island Ferry presses into the choppy mouth of the bay
where sailboats bow down in a struggle against a whistling wind
and geese follow their own long necks through the mantle of fog,

as the Angel Island Ferry presses into the choppy mouth of the bay
where the Miwok once came in with long poles in thin reed boats
past geese following their own necks through the mantle of fog,
where they came for salmon and sea fowl, for leaf and seed.

The Miwok once came in with long poles in thin reed boats,
where Spanish sailors mapped and named the island and inlets,
where there was salmon and sea fowl, seed and leaf and root,
and an infantry on foot took aim to strike down the tribes,

where Spanish sailors mapped and named the island and inlets,
where Chinese paper sons engraved poems on wood barrack walls,
where infantry on foot took aim at and struck down the tribes.
*Like pear blossoms already fallen, pity the branches in late spring,*

the Chinese paper sons engraved upon wood barrack walls,
*A flickering lamp keeps the body company* above the bluffs and cove.
*Like pear blossoms already fallen, pity the branches in late spring.*
*The sad person sits alone, leans by a window,* a paper son wrote,

and a *flickering lamp keeps a body company* above bluffs and cove
where sailboats bow down in a struggle against a whistling wind
and *the sad person sits alone, leans by a window* to track the moon,
and a Chinese couple charts family landings at the map, passes time.

# THE NARRATIVE THREAD

(Villanelle for the Practice of Kanthas)

They stitch as if we need these blankets to crawl under,
these thoughts that toss sweet dreams into fretful nights.
They stitch patches of stories onto a tongue of cloth.

They stitch girls left to sicken, to die, books torn from them,
stitch in women's fisted faces on a stammer of speech.
They stitch as if we need these blankets to crawl under.

They take to needle and thread in a revolution of stitch,
stitch speaking in streets without asking for permission.
They stitch patches of stories onto a tongue of cloth.

They stitch in women veiled at home, poisoned widows,
stitch mango groves to chemical spills, wheat fields to AIDS.
They stitch as if we need these blankets to crawl under.

They stitch girls burned by in-laws at husbands' pyres,
stitch palms ripe with fruit, gang rapes at hands of authority.
They stitch patches of stories onto a tongue of cloth.

They stitch quilts for shoppers to slip under with dreams,
to sleep between borders stitched in a revolution of fingers.
They stitch as if we need these blankets to crawl under.
They stitch patches of stories onto a tongue of cloth.

—*for The Bandit Queen, Phoolan Devi, 1963-2001*

# GHOSTS IN THE GARDEN

(Epistle from The Battery, Charleston, SC)

From the city carriage house, from my window inside the piazza,
from here I think I hear them. And there are two of them moving
about below inside a shuffle of whispers. There is a girlish burst
of giggles lilting Gullah tongues. I imagine them there, charmed
by the night, by desire, hooked in the dark into the crooks
of the arms of their own cavaliers, these brown-skinned girls
in genteel Charleston, girls dreaming twilit promenades
wide enough for sweeps of hooped-skirt fashions in from London,
ample as their gentlemen's gusty promises sweeping the walks,
promises that could lift them swift as evening wind, lift them
with the sudden surprise of thick and musky jasmine sailing in,
their fancies flitting like patches of moonlight fluttering across
oyster shells ground in on the walk, the young heart drifting
with dream and desire.

But at the old Round Church where I propped myself earlier today
in the bright of day against a tree to watch the shadow of a cat lilt
plot to plot, against a sky rumbling low with Charleston's incoming
afternoon rain—this haunts me now: I think I heard
a gravedigger's groan, his shovel hit the ground, imagined him
back bent weary, burying six years of smallpox and yellow fever,
a hurricane, the Yamassee raids, all the nuisances of a noisy history.

And now here above this garden of ghosts dark has fallen into,
my thoughts sweep like bees loosened from night corners in a wild
thrum, darting between here and there, between patchy moonlight
and shadows. And I turn over these clamorous thoughts, try
to bury them in the deep plush of my bed in the room above where
horses once stabled. Where I think I hear a bridled mare, the clips
and clomps of her impatient hooves haunting the night. The night
in which a skirt was hooked in the narrow between the kitchen
and main house, when to be a man of property was enough license
to take a girl against her will, tether her with the fury of his passion,
as someone listened above the garden gate carved in hearts afire,
as someone pressed her hands across her ears, slipped inside
a heavy spell of jasmine wrapping the night, slipped into sleep,
into the unbearable inevitability of her own silence.

# CALENDAR GIRL

(or This is a Poem for My Mother)

This is a poem for my mother. She gave it to me in ballpoint
notes tucked into an envelope marked "the wedding." This is
a poem about a girl with green eyes in a linen and lace dress,
carrying a parasol, pressing button top shoes into coal town
ground, and red rose petals my mother strew at her feet.

This poem is for my mother, in a tizzy and woozy with this girl
with green eyes on a wedding day marrying a lanky man
who might have been called handsome with a different nose.
This poem is about a storybook beauty, protected from work,
who learned to clean on her wedding day when the groom
put a broom in her hands, made her sweep coins tossed
with twigs and dirt onto the wood-planked dance hall floor.

My mother asked me to write this poem. It is for her. It is for
a girl with green eyes carrying a bouquet of homegrown roses,
her picture on the calendar page my mother clipped and tacked
to her bedroom wall. My mother says she will never forget her
eyes like she will never forget her own mother's long brown hair.

# I Have Seen Terezin

(Pantoum from Frankie's on the Divisadero in San Francisco)

The sign at Frankie's Bohemian Café reads *6,303 miles to Prague.*
Inside a shadowed corner I have brambory, rough bread, Pilsner—
the same way I did in the sleepy Bohemian bordertown of Terezin.
I still hear from here mothers' voices, appoggiaturas on the wind.

Inside a shadowed corner I have brambory, rough bread, Pilsner,
think of children painting sprawling meadows, their butterfly skies,
and hear from here mothers' voices, appoggiaturas on the wind.
Now we study this, housefronts tattooed in SS brass plaques,

children painting flowers sprawling meadows, their butterfly skies,
feather quilts airing our sins across the opened window ledges.
Now we study this, housefronts tattooed in SS brass plaques,
the Camp's mass grave's numbered markers bedding down in roses,

feather quilts airing our sins across the opened window ledges,
gallows wreathed in candles, slips of prayers tucked under stones,
the Camp's mass graves numbered markers bedding down in roses
for ones hung at the Gate of Death. I walked tunnels from the cells

to gallows wreathed in candles, slipped prayers beneath stones,
jumping at my own shadow darting by me, at how horror twists it,
at those hung at the Gate of Death. I walked tunnels from the cells,
taunted by its dark angels' voices, quilts and roses, butterfly skies,

jumping at my own shadow darting by me, at how horror twists it,
the way I squared walkways in the sleepy bordertown of Terezin—
taunted by its dark angels' voices, quilts and roses, butterfly skies,
while a sign at Frankie's Bohemian café reads *6,303 miles to Prague.*

—*for Friedl Dicker-Brandeis*

# Altar Piece

Children empty the mother's house of her,
muscles aching from the weight of her loss
held in their arms so close to their hearts.
Light a candle for them.

Neighbors bemoan an old man lost
just blocks from his home.
No one ever reported him missing.
Pray on beads for them.

Strangers, heads darting this way and that,
circle a young man on the tracks who slipped
into a heap crossing the street.
Petition the saints for them.

Light a candle for them.

Light a candle for girls who gave birth
in the dark the way they conceived,
buried stillborns in deep graves of grief.
Bury your face in your hands for them.

And for the parents whose children fell
to open school ground fire, who, uprooted,
wither upon the blood soaked earth.
Lay down wreathes of marigolds for them.

Ring bells for them.

Ring bells for women, pack at the heels
with knife, brick, and pipe, who dropped
in the dark, rapt into sleep, then forgot.
Cover the mirrors for them.

Ring bells for the men who balk
at the buck of the rifle butt, drop guns
and run, rogues cast out from the pack.
Raise flags for them.  Free doves for them.

And for those with bodies bound by rope,
throats gagged with rags, backs strapped
and lashed, their cries silenced.
Open a window for them.

Deliver oblations for them.

For all the apocalyptic visionaries who leapt
to their ends from bridge rails, or slept drunken
on fumes in the room in a blanket of death.
Burn incense for them.

Sing chants at altars you create for them.
Carve their names deep into stone
you erect to them. Let their ashes
take wings on the wind for them.

—*for all the Altaristas*

# IMPRESSIONS EN PLEIN AIR

(from Flight 2199, Regarding Monet)

Far above the street scene graffiti of Paris,
I think of you, Monet, from the air up here
flying this sea foam sky, a shelf of waves
against a floor of mist breaking open
in patches of blue and white.

And I, like some devotee of impending
collisions in texture and transparency, dapple
words as Giverny expatriates might have once
on palettes a harvest of light, cultivating
a poetry of space en plein air.

I have looked, Monet, into the mirror into which
you must have many times glanced or long gazed,
your Orient prints awash in blue flirting the glass
with the constant movement of the sea
in which little else has changed.

You grew big bellied with age, tousle of hair thick
with gray, sight on the wane, canvases growing,
you padding through the long yawn of rooms
painted blue as lichen, yellow as sunflowers,
reflecting lilies afloat between the sky and the water.

But in your garden, beyond the rose blanketed fence,
those flowers brown now in a wilted July. I have looked,
Monet, into the mirror into which you must have
glanced or long gazed recollecting those lilies for me,
yet another tourist here.

They tell me the best part of your life was inhabiting
these gardens. And as the light fades, I cannot help
but wonder where it is next that I will go, and of my words,
what will they become stretching there
*en plein air.*

30

# 3.

*Waiting alone by the sea, hearing the wash of the waves,*
*Learned the secret from them of the beautiful verse elegiac . . .*

—Longfellow

# WE WERE DANCING

(or This Poem is for My Father)
*. . . There is my past which is really past . . .*
—from Guillaume Apollinaire's "There Is"

There are my feet in cotton socks on your toes.
There is a Patti Page waltz, my wing bone arms at your waist.
There I am with you, bathed in light. I hold on tight.
    We are dancing.
There is long ago and long to come.
There is a flutter of leaves on a speechless breeze.
There is a wind moving in, in an echo of motion and chatter.
There are clouds in the sky I search for your face.
There are strangers a blur in the crowd, a hum heavy with voices.

There is who you have become, your face a face in the crowd,
    one of many faces
on a vendor selling lace in a stall at Les Puces de Paris Saint Ouen,
on the lips of a Tunisian eating chorizo at Gare St-Lazare,
on the ferry captain's arms at Pont Neuf along the Seine,
on the soldier riding the train watching sunflowers grapple the fields,
on the old man's hands rolling balls across Coquille Square,
on a gypsy I tossed coins for a look at your amber eyes on his face,
on the Moroccan, Bastille Day, just off Rue St. Antoine. In the street,
    we were dancing.

There are words pressed into my fingertips brushing your cheek.
There is me missing all that you might have become. You are large.
There is you looming above me wrapped by your muscled arms,
    and dancing.
There is your heart beating hard inside my chest wall.
There is time passing through me like a conduit.
There is long ago. There is long to come.
There is this past that is really past.
There is me, suddenly without you.

# My Mother's Legs

*This is the journey of the body, its hesitant footsteps*
*as it walks back into its own flesh. I close my own*
*eyes so I can see better where we are going.*
—from Margaret Atwood's "Hands"

My mother's legs appeared to me
again today. This time in a pivot,
her toes pointed in a brown pump,
calves taut, the way
I first saw them tighten
when she pulled herself up
by my father's shoulders,
under the porch light
when she thought I wasn't looking,
to kiss him on the cheek.

Her legs appeared again
to me. There was a stage.
It was backlit, draped with velvet,
the way she told it, with a banner that read:
*Miss Legs of Mercy Hospital,*
the honor of bed pans, dated magazines,
the job as a nurse's aide.
I thought, of course, they danced.

I saw my mother's legs again,
under the dance hall ball, a flicker
of lights skipping whitewashed walls,
in a marathon where she jitterbugged
a sawdusted floor at a Moose
or the Polish Falcons, with men
sporting vacant stares who let her
lean into the breadth of their chests
and doze for a trophy.

I saw them, they appeared again,
this time switched and welted
by bad boys in Central Park where she walked
alone at dusk seeking the solace of trees.

*Mean*, she said, rubbing the ghost
of their pain from her legs,
some hooligans she never forgot
in stories she repeated to me
about the dangers living away
from home, even escaping her own
father's belt at her legs.

One time I saw them, her legs,
so pink, she on reddened knees
scrubbing the worn kitchen tiles.
*Baby doll legs*, I thought then watching
when she looked up, tossed
the brush back into the soapy pail,
a slosh of suds splashing up at us
as she pulled me into the plush of her
young belly, the soft sweet of her small
breasts, and whispered to me,
*Now don't you run your roller skates*
*across my clean floor.*
And how we giggled then
because she knew I would.

The last time I saw my mother's legs,
they were splayed out from under her.
I could not rub away the cold and pale
and deadly still. I put some slippers
on her feet.
            This is the life she made
            for me to walk into.
            This is the way
            it works now.
            I end up
            on my knees
            on the damp ground, offering
            a simple flurry of mums
            to an altar of earth.

# THE GOOD DAUGHTER SPEAKS OF DEATH IN PLAIN FACT

*There is nothing I have buried that can die.*
—from Adrienne Rich's "Calle Vision"

The dream is always the same. I am lying on my side
on a long, silver table. The clock's hands have stopped,
but I cannot read the time. It is cold, and I am covered
by a thin white sheet. Only my leg is visible. The leg
of a twenty-year-old, the way my mother saw it when
she took to remembering winning contests with her own.
I stand above it, reach down, touch it. The round ball
of flesh that was muscle falls away from the bone
into the cup of my hand. I drop it, and it shatters
as it smacks against the concrete floor.

It is May. And Spring has come lilting in. I am awake.
Yet I am tired. And it is not a dream. It is not my calf,
not my leg. She is there. And alone. In the front room
of the rowhouse. It is her foot at my feet and the slipper
I pick up from where it skidded across the carpet
as she slid on her way pushing herself up from the chair.
On her way to see what was the commotion of children
in the yard. On her way to see if it was me pulling in
at the curb. There is no other way to say this. I found
my mother, dead, on the living room floor.

It is Sunday. I am a day late. My arms full with an apology
of flowers. They are red. Petunias to bloom along her walk,
endure the summer heat that surely would come. I knock,
but there is no answer. I rise up on tiptoes to peek through
the door glass. I see them there, my mother's legs sprawled
out across the floor. She is humped over on her side, knees
buckled under. Her foot, small as any child's, is pale
and limp and bare. Her head bruised in a graze off
an old coal bucket stuffed with souvenirs at the door.
She must have fainted. Her skin is pale. And pasty cold.

Her eyes are closed, the slipper off. I heave under the weight
of her body, shudder at the hurt of it. It is not easy to talk
about death, to talk about her now, her beautiful hands
writing notes to herself so she would not forget some thing,
sending letters across town so that others could not.
I think once, as she suffered my endless questions, I heard her
say, "yes, yes, you are a good daughter," as I was writing out
some other version of myself, one I could live with,
before death would not let her catch her breath once more.

The clouds are low and light and white. I expected that
when it came to this, it would be a night pierced by rain
clawing a wintry sky, me racing a highway of sirens, the way
I practiced it, as if that would be the only way it could come,
bold and dark, in a frenzy, in a storm. But it is quiet. I am
alone, trying to believe she has gone somewhere her body,
fouled by death, cannot go. Her brow is furrowed, eyes are
closed, lips turned downward as if not to want to see this,
me finding her here and wishing that of what I had to give,
there would have been more.

# Unknown Man Dies on Street

This boy, a young man really, dropped to his death
as he stepped down from the car stop into the street
at Market near Third in San Francisco. The sun dimmed.
It was another oddly cool July. He tumbled
into a heap upon the tracks.

Everyone stood still.
He never made it across the street.
He was blond, hair clipped fashionably short. He was tall,
maybe of Nordic stock. He wore pressed jeans. He was clean.
I stood there staring.

Someone must have called someone who wasn't there
yet. He wasn't my friend, my son, anyone I knew
or was obligated to, not my mother who weeks earlier lay
in her own heap in Pittsburgh, pale and limp and cold,
for me to find.

He was a young man, freshly shaven, skin turned ashen.
He was flesh, bone, tracks, cement, a crowd of strangers
circling round, some family off somewhere
about to get the news.

The next streetcar screeched to a halt, sirens close behind
as he lay grade to the street there, and I took him into the dark
recesses of my mind--into a grave, worm eaten, bones
picked clean, bleach-white as roadkill.

Or turned by fire into small chips and shell, me thinking
I can hear my father saying the body being cremated
sits up arms flailed out, eyes popped open, everything
twitching and flinching

like those chickens whose necks he made me watch him wring
down in the basement before, beheaded, they circled round us

again and again in some choreography
of the wild.

And just as I am recalling the dark of that dingy place,
a small boy, maybe seven or eight, tugs at my sleeve,
whimpers, "Lady, lady, will it be alright? What will happen now?"
And I look down at him, put my hand into the soft crop of hair
on his head and tell him it will be alright,
that others have been called to help.
"They'll take care of him?" he says.
"They'll take care of him," I say, his mother standing there,
mouth agape, her eyes flitting between us and the street.

And so, this is why I tell myself I find myself here today
at Third and Market in San Francisco where a young man
has just dropped dead, stepping from the island into the street:

I am here
for this small child,
reminding me of my own boy once, eyes full of terror at a dog
he watched hit by a car, its little body slung helplessly across
the pavement, my own boy, his cheeks a rash of pink, eyes reddened,
hands balled into fists, lip trembling from bullies who badgered him
the long block from a schoolyard to a porch swing
where I told him
it would be
alright.

But this boy, unlike my own,
believes me.

And for this moment in which cars brake and streetcars clack
and clang ahead, I know why I am here. It is for this twist
of time and space and chance. It is for the child,
for this small boy
bearing his first witness
to death.

# CHILD:

At the start you grew
hooked to me,
took shape as you should
in the strange
possibility of permutations.

From my largest cell you did spring,
dividing, multiplying, drifting, shifting,
burrowing in the womb wall. You took shape.
Head and tail, buds of arm, leg, heartbeat,
paddle hands, webbed fingers and toes, my little
ducky, puppy asleep at the base of my spine,
turning on our cord connection, my body
making room for you, my heart growing larger
for you. You must hear this as I rock here
and you have turned to go live outside
my danger zone.

You inhabit me still. I loved you
before you were
large enough to see, loved you
before you were
even an idea.

—*in memory of Miroslav Holub*

# I Thought We Would Survive It All

*. . .You want the final drink.*
*The one before you can't remember.*
*The one that makes you believe*
*there is no pain.*
—Georgeann Eskievich Rettberg
Sept. 1, 1952 - Mar. 24, 2003

I thought we would survive it all,
from duck and cover under classroom desks
in Pittsburgh practicing for the H-bomb
to a polio epidemic and the Cold War,
even our parents' *double shifts in darkness*
*with summer sweat on the necks,*
*winter ice on the hands.* And we did survive
those friends we lost to jungle and desert wars,
bad trips, bar scenes, all the false promises
we could not then comprehend.

I thought we did survive,
across town from each other as girls on tiptoes
at kitchen sinks cranking open spigots to wash
the dopey perfume of our fathers' whiskey
down the drain those Sunday mornings
we hauled trays to our *Kings of Polka,*
cups of black coffee teetering against glasses
of tomato juice topped by raw eggs jiggling
at their rims. And our mothers yelling
to let-them-sleep-it-off, as they left
their *invisible fingerprints in houses they cleaned*
*and polished,* hearts broken on Saturday nights
that cheated them, beset by what they called
women troubles they said as girls
we could never understand.

We survived the long waits as good daughters
easily amused by fireflies sparking dusk,
our chins cradled in our tiny hands,
arms propped up on boney elbows, waiting
for crab apples we caught in our skirt hems
to be turned into pies oozing over with sweet,
before starving ourselves thin courting
the cruel beast of beauty, force-fed
what we would not digest.

We survived as steelworkers' daughters
the hard toe of the sooty boot, the strap
clutched in drunken fists, *fighting off their snakes*
*with the anger of our bloody fingers.*
We survived hard living and long deathbeds
*in the charcoal smoke of Pittsburgh*
*spreading between the front gate*
*and walk to the furnace, the cough choking*
*the ash inside* them. We even survived
being sent off for respectable teaching jobs
into classrooms swollen with Ritalin babies,
their furbies, beanies, and lolitot fashions,
bruised eyes squinting at each day's conundrums,
camouflaged by grins of cartoon proportions.

We survived our retreats with mad poets
and bad fortune tellers, the instructions
on how to survive *coming of age with our thighs*
*breathing the fire of hands,* survived
Pollyanna predictions for our lousy lovers,
bad dancers, and other assorted lost causes,
whiskey perfuming their breath.

But you would not survive that last drink,
*the one before you can't remember.*
It is not easy to survive. It is not easy
to be left behind to make meaning
of a gun sloppy in your mouth, to imagine
the swift click of the trigger, explosion,
silence, dead week's stay on the morgue slab
flagged with a toe tag, your body
misshapen and gaunt, a pornography of living,
everyone averting their eyes.

Today the moody air, like these words,
seems tentative and muggy and gray,
seeking out a harbor, some safety
where this storm of you can buffer
then pass like nights that break on the ease
of incoming dawn. Today I survive,
wedding the fragrance of myrrh to a flicker of light,
fingering beads on an old catechism rosary.

You would call this an altar of memory
constructed for you, as I try to make
some meaning from this *like furnace fire,*
*like whiskey energy,* with you on my mind
*yelling and singing, moving to the step*
*of a Saturday night polka, your voice*
*in perfect pitch with the band.*

# THE ANNIVERSARY OF MY MOTHER'S DEATH NEARS AND ANOTHER WAR HAS COME AND GONE

*Reality demands*
*That we also mention this:*
*Life goes on.*
—from Wislawa Szymborska's "Reality Demands"

It's the same
old story.
Another body is going into the ground today.
It is somebody's mother. A daughter weeps
for the wrap of the arms that once stilled
her trembling body in their firm hold on her.
It's the same old story. Another war
is going on again, this one twenty-five years past
the fall of Saigon, missiles behind, explosions
inside. Men suit up like boys again
in flak jackets for the media blitz,
and there are wars
going on all over.

The rituals
continue.
We light candles, the kind that burn
seven days. We don't question these acts.
We get on our knees like martyrs, like beggars,
heads bent like priests, say prayers, go
to the wall with our pain, wrestling
our need to be here. We bury our faces
in our hands, lament cross deeds, swallow sobs.
We move on, negotiating mine fields everywhere
where the story takes
the same twist.

Some stranger
extends a hand to you,
says he's sorry for your long suffering
in the relentless face of death, so you
lift yourself from your knees, look off
beyond the grave toward the river the future
courses through, reshaping contours
of the world, and for a moment it seems
to slow, grow glassy, come in  closer to you,
your eyes a blur and trying to follow where
it might lead, when the gravedigger's shovel
hits the ground in a thud, while you become still,
watch him rub the small of his back.

# THIS:
# A TRIPTYCH FOR THE DISAPPEARED

> *Her face has disappeared. This happens*
> *more often than you think . . .*
> —from Andrea Hollander Budy's "Woman in the Painting"

## 1.

She is six.
She is a kid
in a cowgirl suit,
strapping on a holster
at her cherry three-wheeler,
the city steed, clumps of mud
in the ring of its chain.
But it has come to this:

Twenty years later
she is on her back,
a woman dressed up
as someone's bed,
blood on the sheets.
She is the bed,
She is the ceiling,
She is the wall,
She is the room.

This has happened:
Her face disappeared
beneath the scarlet
throb of a bruise.

## 2.

This is the country where
nothing sells for more
than its whores, rest
and recreation for a global
economy, pedophiles reclined
behind a camouflage of pc screens,

eagerly scanning rental lists
by the hour, by the day,
by the month, for a lifetime,

the sexual slavery pimp's finger
on the trigger of the cocked
crack gun, lolitot posed
like a CK ad in a flickering
lightbulb dark, catalogued
child-bride, ready-made to order,
but she is not this body. *This*
is not a good job for a poor girl.

## 3.

Across the sprawling green of lawn
at another Dias de Los Muertos,
pink crosses stagger the walk
for the murdered women of Juarez,
hundreds disappeared over a decade.

A procession of candles sputter
and spark for a school house splattered
in blood, its Amish girls gunned downed
by a milk truck driver with three guns
and a grudge in West Nickel Mines, PA.

Muffled prayers petition the October air
for women packed tight in shipping containers
across the Pacific Northwest, later to appear
on packing lists masked as menus, their bodies
indexed as lo mein, satay, kimchi, pho.

Frankincense smolders for those who
vanish, shadows in the streets, whole bodies
disappearing under the weight of burqas.
It burns for all of those who are not,
for all of those who never will be.

—*for Mayra Juliana Reyes Solis, Juarez Cotton Fields sex murder victim*

# WHEN ONE MORE ELEGY WILL NOT DO

*...Among these landscapes the poor soul winds,*
*vanishes, returns, approaches, recedes,*
*A stranger to itself, evasive,*
*At one moment sure, the next unsure of its existence ...*
—from *Torture* by Wislawa Szymborska

**1.** day after day in the sunlit hours, all day
inside the emptied house haunted by the body
I watched at its work, the body's hands
tuning in the radio for some news, shuffling
through notes of what next there was to do,
pasting photographs onto pages of memory,
the body's memory occupying the single chair
at a table cleared of stories spilled across it,
cleared of stories that could have come, of those
that might have inhabited the emptied house
in sunlit hours, filled now by an afterlife
after her and inhabited only by her absence.

**2.** inside the emptied house in the sunlit hours,
day after day, year after year where I went
to be of some use, scrub the tub, carry in food
change the drapes, shake the rugs, take out trash,
inside the small and emptied parcel of space I once
decorated with holiday bows is a dead woman's home,
my homemade soups and sauces in the freezer still,
the bed unmade, her plate and glass at the sink,
as if she would get to it soon, and the instructions
are there, the notes of what to do with her body
on this day she said must surely come, and did.

**3.** as daylight hours fade and the emptied house
dims within a waning light, only shadows remain
of what was saved inside the house stripped bare
of its small and ordinary treasures, the small pleasures
of everyday living stacked on shelves, hung up high,

47

tucked in drawers, saved for a day when they might be
of some use, but like idle thoughts now lifeless lay
boxed inside a melancholic moonlight, boxed inside
this shell of mortar and brick, sobs the songs
night sings inside a house emptied of her where I burn
candles for all the souls of my dead, watch them dance
the fiery tips in a fevered display flecked onto walls.

**4.** above the emptied house, the sky's dim jewels
a gaudy light lead morning round to where I stand
and stare, unexpected as the stranger I have become
to myself, bleary-eyed reflection in her mirror
from where I will travel far away to be yet make a plea
as if she can be petitioned by prayer, like some god
of mythological proportion, and I beg an answer
to the prayer I make on bent knee inside the house
in plaintive half-light as I call upon all the blessings
I thought I bought at cathedrals for her weak heart,
flying between cities like they were poems in a book
under construction, like this life under revision.

**5.** as I move further from the emptied house
and sunlit days, I think I hear her here and there,
at my arm stepping into Pittsburgh traffic, hear her
warnings washing over Youghiogheny rapids,
her calls inside an Appalachian countryside,
her starlit whispers haunting Charleston gardens,
my name sung on the trill of birds in sweet
Seattle after rain, hear her say upon wind
above Chicago lakeshore to fix my eyes upon the sky,
hear her down the Western coast where shorebirds dip
and dive, and cry and cry and cry.

**6.** far from the house emptied of her, by candlelight
a circle of women sing a capella at the wake, sing
against the war inside mournful hearts anchored
in silences strung between clumsy exchanges about afterlife.
all I know of afterlife after her is that mine is occupied
by her absence, that I will live through the long low dreaded
peal of funeral bells echoing the hills, the rivers, the sky,
my suffering heart stilled only by the struggle to ascribe
some meaning to this, some meaning greater than this
grievous moment lying endless before me has become
in the deceptive sunlight, haunted by her, by the idea
that heaven is only made from what we once were.

# TRYING TO RAISE THE DEAD

I want you to say it    my name    and slowly
not fast    as you read my note here    bent
characters that    click    tick    in a pesky
night clock    I want to hear it    my name
haunt the stairs tonight    in thin whispers
of wind    trembling in    I want my name
to rattle your tongue    with I am sorry
I didn't mean to    I won't    not ever again
I didn't know    what I was doing    out there
in the drunken moon    inside-out    wrong

I want to hear    my name    fix itself upon
the bruised swell    of this    up all night
cried too deep    half sleep hurt    I could
forgive you    anything    if I would hear you
say it    so I won't    forget    myself
in the dark here    in the fall air    stiffening
into the tap   and clack   of bare twigs against
the raised window glass    say it    so I won't
die alone    inside tonight    my hands bloody
kneading    this heart    back to life.

# It Was Then I Kissed Her

The sky a flutter of birds
just before the day turned dark,
　　she sometimes might be sitting,
　　sometimes might be reading something,
　　a Conrad or Faulkner novel, something
　　she salvaged from thrift shop stacks.

The night a clamor of crickets
rubbing their wings in early dark,
　　she sometimes might be sitting,
　　sometimes writing something,
　　long letters in fine points of memory
　　traveling short distances, just across town.

The nightbirds rioting the green of trees,
a cacophony of crickets under an indigo sky,
　　she sometimes might be complaining
　　about something, those next door kids
　　out too late, the plot of grass she paid
　　to have mowed turned a dried mud patch.

The crickets almost a deadening drone,
Nightbirds a mutter settling into the trees,
　　I sometimes might be leaning into her then
　　to kiss her quickly on her cheek,
　　she most times pulling back, shooing me off
　　like some unexpected junebug grazing the face.

And night birds would flutter the trees,
and crickets would rub in the dark,
and kids would go in for their beds,
and the book would close in on its leaves,
and letters would be licked shut,
and she would frown when she thought
I wasn't paying attention to something.

And neither of us would ever admit
it was not much longer for this kind of living,
and then when the sky went really dark,
and the birds were really quieted,
and the crickets stopped their wild song,
    then, for the first time,
    in her casket,
    I kissed her hard
    and on the mouth.

# At the Obon

(thinking again of you, Mother.)

I saw you at Obon Festival in Japantown
in San Francisco where you have never been,
saw you in the eyes and on the smiles of women there
wearing the bleached moonface you wore near the end
in the emergency room from overmedication. Someplace else,

in Osaka maybe, we could have dispatched you
with the old ways to the heavens on chants of Buddhist monks,
or cremated you in Tokyo where we could later retrieve
the sand and shelly fragments of you from a conveyer belt
with a bar code and credit card. Some other time,

far into the future, keep you in a display of dry ice,
or dancing on laser beams for holographic reproduction.
Here women made up like geishas dance the Bon Odori,
circle drums, their wraiths from candles and lanterns aglow,
and with your face in my eyes, I pray with them

that we might really flee this path of hungry ghosts
they ward off, and suffer no more.

# 4.

*If one woman told the truth about her life,*
*the world would split open.*

—Muriel Rukeyser

# Swimming Lessons

The first time around I did it all,
the buoyant back float, fishy underwater scoot,
cutting the surface with scissor legs, breathing
and bobbing, readying for the day of the dive,
the big test,
a life saving badge.

That first time, I lined up with the best of the rest,
white capped in blue suits, flat chests barreling out,
limbs stretched tall as pride at the board. Springing,
the cold rattle of steel echoing off bathhouse tile,
I took my dive
and a belly smacker.

Twenty years later at the faith healer's where I went
with shallow breath and a nervous stomach
for a second opinion, she told me never oh never
learn to swim, to stay away
from water and bridges
where death would tow me under.

But in my dreams
I am swimming.
It is raining.
I go for the curl
inside the wave.
I come up floating,
breathing and bobbing.
The sun is shining.
In my dreams
I am dying
for water.

# Bittersweets for Camellia

*Segregation of white and colored children
in public schools has a detrimental effect . . .*
—Chief Justice Earl Warren, Brown v Board of Education

The classroom air choked with chalk dust
and floor wax, but huddled in close outside
on the fire escape landing at West Park School
in McKees Rocks, we tasted chocolates plucked
from inside the heart-shaped Russell Stover box
where my mother hid her bonbons—
*a bite for you, a bite for me.* The Baby Ruths
from the corner candy store cost you
your milk money, Camellia, the outside melt
the color of your hands, the nougats and creams
inside light as my fingertips breaking into the chew.

We hummed our sticky sweet delights stowed inside
our Butterick jumper pockets, until the teacher
flagged me across the stretch of cement school yard
over to the iron gate that led back to your row house
and my tenement, across hopscotch lines chalked in—
a clumsy journey, swings clanging against
a school bell ringing in the end of play for the day.

*Don't do that,* the teacher whispered
like a secret, like a sin, words that traveled
from a playground of a schoolhouse long razed
in Pittsburgh all the way to Charleston
one springtime where in the Old Slave Market
I plucked from a ballast of stone a camellia,
a scentless bloom that fell apart in my hands,
flew in a flurry of spent petals into the wind.

*Don't do that,* words that confounded children
in the Sunflower State finally able to walk together
to school, or those giggling under cherry blossoms

facing the sprawl of Capitol monuments, or others
digging toes in sand on the Chesapeake Bay
sharing a peach—*a bite for you, a bite for m*e.

Or evenings, their chins perched on hands,
listening together in the quiet to nightingales
flowering the dogwood—but this bothers me now:
Camellia, the last time I was in Pittsburgh
so many years after, I saw you boarding
the 14C back to West Park, arms brimming
with McCrory store bundles, a little
light-skinned girl latched to your waist,
and I stood there frozen to the curb, unable
to wave my hand, unable to raise my voice,
dumbstruck by words drifting in from a teacher
whose face or name I cannot recall:
*Don't do that*, she said, its bittersweet
still on my tongue.

# Hearts and Diamonds

(or the Lesson of the Gypsy Tea Room
in Tasseography and Cartomancy)

Those Saturday afternoons of window shopping
were the future dressed up as a beaded dress
hanging in the Gimbel's window display,
or a milky scarf draped over a steamer trunk
at Joseph Hornes with trinkets of travel—
pink champagne heels, smart brocade bag
sporting a ticket out to someplace-else-not-here.

Saturdays, before a sleepy matinee
at the Warner Theatre for *Breakfast at Tiffany's*
or *Splendor in the Grass*, we traveled
past the blast furnace layoffs, pig iron
and molten steel of our parents' lifelines
in Pittsburgh, entered the muted narrow of hall,
climbed two flights up and over the shoeshine parlor
in Market Square, up to the Gypsy Tea Room,
the two of us giddy with expectation.

Lunch money in our change purses, we were ready
to pay for what we wanted to hear, the price no more
than the cost of little sandwiches trimmed down
to white triangles smeared with egg salad
we ate fast to get to a scoop of orange sherbet,
dusty almond tea cakes on the side, all delivered
on plates we thought surely *good* china.
Then, of course, there was *the tea*.

Three swirls of the cup to predict secrets
of love, fortune, luck, to reappear as hearts and diamonds
on common playing cards those magical Saturdays
on the heels of long weeks of hall passes,
feigned illnesses in a school nurse's office,
civics classes skipped for Coca Cola and chips
at Isaly's Dairy in West Park, filling the time
between Saturdays. It was spring. We were sixteen.
We wanted something we called *more*, wanted it now.

We sipped our steeped tea slowly from dainty cups,
ribbons of laced florets worn thin at the lips, watched
leaves settle into blurs we conjured into foggy constellations
of stars we hoped the gypsy fortune tellers would see,
hearts athrob with promise of weddings to handsome,
hard working stiffs who would make it back
from a desert war, put rings on our fingers,
give us all the bread and roses of our needs.

The fortune tellers, all named Marie, wore bouffants
matted into stiff caps of fashion, the tasseographers
and cartomancers, our Queens of Hearts,
their long red nails tapping cards as if to get their attention
and ours away from slim cigarettes we nervously puffed,
anticipating something yet to be, something we might
yet become, spellbound by a desperation to grow up,
to grow into someone else's life, to get out, get away.

Today, so many years after and a coast away,
yet like a child adept at passing time, I became
starry-eyed again, this time from the sun
as I decorated clouds with patterns of girlish ways
when a white pelican flew overhead, hauling
its ancient structure of bones, as if defying gravity,
to where I saw ghosts of ourselves looking upward
and onward, crouched in a heart shaped cloud,
diamonds in light shards crossing the sky.

In the tea room, we learned little from words
we posed as questions, postured as wishes,
learned even less of loving or living on the journey
into ourselves. We did not know then the idea of ourselves
could dissolve like fog or mist or clouds
into an unseen thing, that at the heart of the matter,
we could have really lived
like there was no tomorrow.

*—for Julianne, long time friend*

# Evolutionary Thoughts

*I feel like a child who while playing by the seashore*
*has found a few bright colored shells . . . while the whole*
*vast ocean of truth stretches out almost untouched and*
*unruffled before my eager fingers.*
—Sir Isaac Newton

When the biology teacher broke out the new textbooks
in our eleventh grade classroom, my thoughts ran rife
across its pages, almost delirious with the notion
I may not have been generated from a mere rib bone
of a man made in an invisible almighty god's image.

Fresh vocabulary poked around in my mouth:
*chromosomal, double helix, empirical observation.*
Then suddenly, even a local scandal made some sense,
how the new parish priest could run off to Montreal
with the Mother of Sorrow's poor box alms
and our school's pretty valedictorian.

I even found myself musing at my own grandmother's
toothless face, monkey-like, shriveled in her old age
on her death bed, all now just part of the scheme of things,
new words on my tongue: *heredity, variation, natural
selection*, everything hooked on evolutionary thoughts.

Dizzy on a slant of dust-flecked light cutting across
the classroom desk in Pittsburgh, with the flip of each
slick text book page, creationism went on trial and lost,
and although the case was not closed, enough of that jury
was in for me—banished was my god of butterfly wings
and banished was my god of blazing penance.

But some things are short-lived as creationists
belt intelligent design back into the courtrooms,
trying Darwin again in Kansas, Ohio, Georgia,
while grad students in Carnegie Mellon think tanks
play air hockey with humanoid robots, debating
with a fury, their rights beyond the laboratory doors.

61

# Mating Season

The ducks are driving me crazy, at it again in the grass,
in the fountain in a splash, and there's that one
the apartment house manager is scooting out the door.

No one seems to think much of this wild pursuit, duck
dragged down, pushed underwater or onto the sand,
feathered courtiers standing watch until their turn.

Small boys, their kites decorating the heavens, ribbon
girls stuffing cuffs of their sleeves full with crab shells
the needle-nosed shorebirds picked through.

But it is these ducks that are driving me crazy, breath
squeezed from one that stumbles then flops under
the next one's mount, then right at my feet preens, rakes

the ribs of her feathers clean, preens them from her.
And now this nosy tern wild-eyes me as I wade away
from them, away from the noisy architects of sandcastles,

toward that one cloud pinned like a gardenia to a pale placket
stitched in pinks and blues to this storm worn sky,
the weather hovering,
          and everything
                    about to change.

# Weather Report from Seaside Hotel

*Now through night's caressing grip*
*Earth and all her oceans slip . . .*
—from W. H. Auden's "Nocturne"

I'm fading tonight, even more quickly than this sky
going dark as cinder, while a roughneck boy with his dog
is fired up on the beach, leapfrogging driftwood and rocks.

I wonder whether they will later lay themselves down
on a gritty bed of sand, flattening their history of footprints,

whether they will curl into each other and rest, whether
their mutual dreams will revisit the raucous of day
detailing the simplicity of feet, of paws kicking up sand.

And just outside the window, the drunken lovers return,
are at it again, stumbling in on too much wine and new raw.

And the waves are roaring in across the way, predictable
how no one will sleep deeply through this night's grip
with the boom and bang of sea on sand at high tide.


Someday I will return to to this blustery place, settle in,
protected from the whip of wind, when I may dream to be

a child running carefree along the beach with a dog,
mastering the simple formula of wild, but for now
I make watch of this spread of sky for signs of storm,

veiled behind a thin curtain of fog, shadows dancing
in the uncertainty of what cannot be forecast.

# After

*I make cries like a bird; I give out sounds of grief like a dove.*
—Isaiah 38:14

after
the cranky caw of the backyard crow,
after geese bellow their offbeat evening refrains,
after thieving herons squawk and beat wings nest side,
after night turns into a still life, city side, lake side,
its clutch of gray clouds lying low in the long summer
on its last breath, night nuzzling into the grassy hills,
perfect lick of light still at the water's edge,
after descending into a rocky, watery sleep,
on the low drone of a cajun fiddle on the radio,
the smell of ash in the air in another fire season,
after this,

there is a woman
screaming in the night,
her garbled tongue spilling onto the stage of the street,
backlit by the steady flash of police car lights,
the shrill of her dampened only by sirens on the scene,
and then the slam of the cruiser's door,
and then the key turning over its ignition,
and then the hum of the motor, then the sudden quiet,
the street finally at rest beneath a halo of misty lamplight,
after

a woman screaming, screaming
like the cat on the fence screeching in heat,
like a fist to a face or a rape, like a war zone,
like a womb ruptured in child birth,
or a mourner's yowl graveside, or some harpy,
or the baby next door waking for its four a.m. feeding,
the neighbor's shepherd barking at the muffled wail
under the milky light of the cracked half-plate moon,
late train in the distance pressing past the square
into the blurry shadows toward some comfort ahead
as I stay on, straightjacketed into insomniac silence

after
a woman screaming in the night
and around whose dark absence
I throw my arms.

# Out of Control

(or The Story of My Life in One Dream and Thirteen Lines)

The road is never the same, never the same,
but the dream is, its ribboning s-curves
snaking bends and thin berms without guardrails,
foot at the gas instead of the brake,
fast enough to wheel into sky,
into its breathy blinding blue
taut canvas stippled by clouds,
the next scene a black screen
peppered with pixels of stars and flying
the mountain, valley, meadow, a range,
axle snapping, wheel locking, but flying
into sky cracked open by sun. Someone
is driving. It is not me. It is not me.

# Turning a Train of Thought Upside Down (or What We Learn)

*. . . as a woman, I have no country. As a woman, I want no country.*
*As a woman, my country is the whole world.*
—from Virginia Woolf's *Three Guineas*

Under the bottle brush tree
the lovers sit, circled in each other's
arms, all alone right in front of us all
on our walks around the city lake,
their kisses blind to the afternoon
breathing down on them and us.

I think of my own first love,
how a woman can learn not to take
but to give, how not to gain a self
but to lose one inside another—
natural as breathing, to be in exile
under her own skin, colonized
without knowing she was occupied.

Long ago, women in my family carried
bundles of wash on their backs
down to the creek bed to scrub it clean,
later balanced books on their heads
for good posture and the possibility
of a cover shot on a fashion magazine,
having been fed a diet of Cinderella,
Sleeping Beauty, the Snow White tales.

Just look at the statistics—how many
of us have sported the split lips,
bruised eyes, broken limbs,
how many assaulted and betrayed,
how many isolated and afraid,
our homes gone up in flames
from so many hearts on fire.

Yet we have resisted and rebelled,
conquered enemies, negotiated peace.
We have also had our feet bound,
bodies girdled and gagged, some buried
beneath layers of cloth. We have been
overthrown, dispossessed, imprisoned,
enslaved, burned wholesale at the stake.

And we have been venerated and feared—
as Congolese leading warriors into battle
with shields and spears, as Mongolians
riding steeds armed with bows and arrows,
as Seneca ruling the land and the clan,
drumming and healing, as Balkans singing
in the company of women, just for the song.

Some of us now build muscles in our legs
and take to running for the thrill of the race,
work them in our arms wielding swords
and wrestling whatever might confront us.
We grow strong enough to carry ourselves
to a shade tree, rest beside the fairy dusters
in the kiss of our own breath, learn to love
first ourselves, deeply, and with great abandon.

# WORRY BEADS

●

Walking home to a new flat in a warm autumnal dusk,
everything crisp and at attention, the gardener packing up
his weekly gear, I can't help but smile at the strong stucco face
topping a leg of a climb uphill, at its odd widow-walk balcony,
and think as I peek through my own open blind slats—how pretty
the eucalyptus bunched in the vase, how tidy a run of temple gates
framed above the mantle, the season's persimmon and pomegranate
centered in a bowl, how sweet the chime of shorebirds singing
in the light breeze, thin linen billowing at the lifted sash.

How I heard once a rapist say he picked his victims by the pretty
through their windows, picked blooms from their flower boxes
when they were not looking, picked them from the neat upkeep
of their lives, hinge plates undone before the latched door.

● ●

I spend the next day between gallery walls for Dias de los Muertos
and thread together beads of memory with marigolds I collect
to attract spirits, incense to guide souls, salt to dry tears, water
to cleanse open wounds, bread of the dead topped with sweet
jimmies. My friend cannot understand why I do not join him
at Techno Cosmic Mass, go trance-dancing. Another won't let up
on trying to coax me onto a target range, practice shooting pistols.

At home, I open all the ground-floor windows, let in the sound
of first rain after long drought, listen to it wash the walk clean.

● ● ●

The woman on the tv show says she explained her breast cancer
to her three-year-old on paper with pencil as an erasable dust fleck
inside a word balloon. During radiation, she visualized this carbon smear
as an end stop on an invisible sentence beam of light. After the mastectomy,
she wished she had earlier followed directions on the placard hung
in the shower stall for touching herself intimately and often.

69

I stop to touch myself, but do not. I light candles instead
for all my dead. *Don't worry*, I tell myself. *Don't worry.*


• • • •

My son is about to have another birthday. I no longer tell his age,
part vanity, part principle. I do not explain my own growth
into this life with him, child with child, his great head still pushing
through me, me strapped to that birthing table like a madwoman
who does not scream but breaks a small bone in the nurse's hand
as the epidural needle jerks into the spinal cord in an untimely
contraction, afraid I would never do another arabesque, and did not.

I imagine the woman who inhabited the next bed still cradles
her sack of a belly absent of the stillborn child. We, strangers
waking to check each other in the shadows of medication, shared
a room and a fleeting promise never ever to forget each other.


• • • • •

At the college where I have taken on teaching writing, a young man
the age of my son flaunts his penchant for synecdoche. My mind
grows hungry for the kitchen chopping board with beets, blood oranges,
strong mince of garlic and zest. I tell him make a poem, not a word game,
as a sugar skull crystallizes at the end of my pen. Another tells me
she can no longer see straight, is huddling again in the jungle in Laos
at her mother's skirt as the house is searched for her father. She tells me
she is suffering. *Don't worry*, I say, *Don't worry. Don't worry.*

The next day I track a hawk in my camera lens from Nimitz Trail,
and into the frame flies a military plane with helicopter escorts
circling the Bay Bridge in the distance. We all worry.

• • • • • •

I organize my new walk-in closet by blacks, grays, the dark blues,
various shoes ranging from frivolous to sensible, and in this array
of San Francisco uniforms resurrect a Sicilian woman I remember
back in Pittsburgh, who wore black throughout her daughter's
teenage years, mourning the loss of her young Roman husband.

All of us drag queens of the dark, I think, working this life
like slaves to the dead, an occasional bauble catching some light.

• • • • • • •

I follow a New Neighbor Welcome Brochure around the city lake
wearing its incandescent halo of pearls—3,400 bulbs to be exact,
punctuated periodically by over 100 Florentine lamp standards—
loop around this bit of a Pacific flyway with its watery feasts,
its silenced wild, settling in an evening mesh of heron, egret,
the ring-billed gulls full of their feed on mussels and tubeworms.

Nights, when I toss between various frets of the noisy music
of the brain, make shopping lists for melatonin and apologies
for not giving anyone what they really want, I sometimes toy
with shaving off my hair to show off a thick skin of eyes tattooed
at the back of my head watching out for something yet to come
when the clock's hands dip downward, when thieves creep in,
and for which no strand of worry beads nor line of poetry
can ever be enough.

## Losing the Balance

*Let it sing!*—Hopi Elder driving up Third Mesa
to a woman trying to stop the dash board rattle.

I like it. I like the rock, the bump, the clunk
of the washer off balance from an extra towel.
I like the clang of its righting itself
in an automatic feature included in the price.

I like its warm when I press my impatience
up against the last minutes of an extra spin.
I like that warm of strange bedfellows:
metal and flesh, motor and pulse.

I even like the way when I close my eyes
in its wind-down hum, I hear the tick tick
of my old wind-up clock, hear the click
of a furnace kicking in on cold eastern nights.

Above the rock and bump and clunk of it,
I like the rock dove's coo, crow's caw caw caw,
honk of geese across the western flyway,
terns laughing it up, the morning opening up.
I like it. I am here. And I like it.

# 5.

*Truly, the only gift you have to give is your own transformation.*
—Lao Tzu

# War Babies

This is it. The place where they met. 1945. America
is warming up with Quaker Oats and toast. Iwo Jima
is falling. The boys are coming back from *over there*
in blues and greens, silver and gold burnishing chests.
I see my mother there. She sits on the sideline.

She studies shorthand to move up from the punch press
to bookwork, since one girl fell to steel an overhead crane
let loose. It is good money, steady work, a small outfit
of immigrants gone big. They get the orders out, turn
feed and cattle cars into munition and artillery hauls.

My father plays ball. He's one of them, waiting out orders
to rivet or weld as girls giggle and watch between lumber
yard stacks and lunch whistles. He swings a bat
at lightning bolt speed. The ball strikes her breast.
He lifts her from her knees. It is love-at-first-sight.
An A-bomb explodes silence across the Southwest.

It is cold out here in this sibylline light. New owners
run a forging plant. The railyard is frozen along her old Ohio.
Rusted sheet-metal ramparts curl out where I peek inside
a time before I was. Truman sends over B-29's. The sun
seems to crawl closer to the earth. Everyone falls in love.

I am about to be conceived. I will fight against the birth
walls. They will take me from my mother's *twilight sleep*.
Other women will rock away my cries, her milk gone
to her head and soured. She'll stay on the job for someone
who will not come back. It will take me years to know her.

# Somedays, Docked Here

(at South Shore Park, Pittsburgh, PA)

All summer we watched
for something, the return
of gulls riverside, ducks
circling boat wakes,
a promise of rain.
We waited like a still life,
butterflies skirting weeds
at our feet, waited
for the rock dove's coo,
a fingernail moon.

Somedays, like house wrens,
we chipped the sticky air
with curious chatter,
dipped and preened,
turned our wings
from the sun, landlocked
by another summer, the pulse
and shift of each other.

Somedays our thoughts bared
and spare as winter limbs,
rose like a surprise,
cheeky and loud
on the wings of geese
beating against the gray of sky
awash with clouds.

One day, at the other side of day,
our eyes blurred by stars,
we breathed in outer space,
and our mouths formed words
the shape of love, and the sky
cracked open with rain blades
sheathed in thunder, electrified
by light, by another simple act
of tension.

# Somebody is Breathing Inside Me

*Somebody is breathing inside me—Birds, the very earth.*
—Shinkichii Takahashi

This is the season of blowzy clouds,
of walking headlong into a western wind
the sun dipping deep into autumn,
trees dropping tresses at dusk
in a rustle of russet to blanket the ground.

This is the season of an improbable journey,
ragged and somber, seeking the shelter of bluffs,
winging the night winding down seaside roads,
mist laden mountains bejeweled by moon,
redwoods arched over the ridge.

Each night now since I winged my way away
from the burden of death's dark silence
in my arms, I crawl in under night covers,
enter dreams, stumble and start, bleary-eyed
and wild, walking headlong into wind.

This is the gift I must give to myself,
to never suffer another deadly winter,
to embrace instead the ribbons of birds,
their new speech blazing like a wildfire
unleashed on the rise.

This is my season. This is the landscape
I have let into my soul, the prospect
of it almost too much to bear—
to begin living again
like lightning without rain.

# THE PICKERS

*Stronger and stronger, the sunlight glues*
*The afternoon to its objects . . .*
from Charles Wright's "Against the American Grain"

The pickers, backbent and dozens abreast, rise before the sun
   past the blonde grasses, behind the concertina wire
running between Soledad and Salinas, move in squats,
   toss artichokes from sun-pocked fields into pickup cabs,
   calloused fingers pricked by the thorny thistles.

They pour seeds into rivulets of dry earth
   that will burst  into lettuce, chard, the great bouquets
   of broccoli and cabbage along El Camino Real's humpback hills
where foremen watch, arms folded across their dusty boredom
   and the long light of days stretching inside another summer.

Bodies at work, long after limbs tire, long after chests heave
   beneath bird-bone beads, abalone shells, scapulars dangling
   from red strings, or even chains of gold glinting off the sun,
   faces muffled in scarves and hoods, sweat scenting the air,
backbent and dozens abreast, birthing a history of earth.

And so they move, the pickers, silhouetted against the horizon,
   westerly winds crossing groves and vineyards farther north,
   farther south, they move, follow the crops, follow the seasons,
Steinbeck's ghost among the harvest gypsies in the fields,
   pen in one hand, pail in the other, working towards some end.

As sure as low clouds cool the day down, the bodies turn
   toward evening, lay down the ache of the field in the stretch of legs,
   slope of shoulders, move toward dreams of the unburned, pain-free,
   unafraid, unspent paper in the pocket for some half-hold on a home
   on the road, birds skittering tree branches at sunset,
   pecking at the unpicked.

# Waiting for Sunset

(at Capitola-by-the-Sea,
on another anniversary)

Waiting for sunset on the sands
at Pleasure Beach, a single sailboat
drifts in along the horizon line.
At cliff's edge, the cypress shadow
umbrellas us where a lone tern
routinely picks through kelp.

We pop the champagne cork,
toast the early evening's spread—

this billow of clouds crossing
the blur of blue sky like a span
of wing bars on the rush of waves
tuning up the night's voice,
droning out our growing quiet
tugging so hard at the tide.

# CONSIDER THE MOON

Consider the moon, how it braids the backroad
   with streamers of light.
Suppose we are stumble-drunk with sweet talk
   in that melancholic dark.

Imagine how loud the sky, bumping between us
   on a bullfrog's groan.
Imagine how we steady our unsure upward climb,
   linked arm-in-arm.

Consider that moon, how it trails our shadows,
   eclipses our walk.
Imagine any Indian Summer night, shivering in
   before a first frost.

Imagine the birds, folding themselves into the pines
   and stark hills.
Suppose everything is shrouded with sleep
   beneath a tipsy moon.

Consider that moon we leave behind to wheel
   its ragged mountainside.
Imagine the two of us, gleaning our way
   under its spell of light.

Imagine a kiss, cheeks blushed by a brush of wind.
   Consider the moon.

# Light Splashed

*... I can scarcely wait till tomorrow*
*when a new life begins for me,*
*as it does each day, as it does each day.*
—from Stanly Kunitz's "The Round"

In that Paris flat we rented that whole month of July
to escape the gray haze routine of our days in Pittsburgh,
in that flat in Paris, light splashed over the stone patio wall,

light seeped across the wood planked sitting room floor
to where we slept curled into each other. Light kissed
leggy geraniums in a flush of pink each side of the doors.

Light bathed them and us in a blush that could only be Paris.

And there at the small square table where we put our cups
of red wine down, ate tarts fat with berries and cream,
we would watch the sun trade its place with the moon.

And there we would sit by candlelight, listen to the *tra la la,*
*la la la* of neighborhood girls, punctuated by their laughter.
That was Paris, a month of summer days filled with light,

each day rising like a new life in the light of another morning

with the stray cat, Doudou, slipping in through the door
purring for a plate of milk and my nails to rake his back
as you slept curled into yourself, Madame next door singing

as she did at the break of each day: *Sous le ciel de Paris.*

Under the sky that was Paris, I'd route our bright days
by rowboat, on foot, from park benches, past grave stones,
mapping out the possibilities of another day:

picnic across some  green, scour a marche de puces for art,
carry a bouquet to a grave, light candles for all our dead,
and we would lead our lives this way for a time

feeding the cat, charting maps, watching sun trade place
with the moon. Now I can barely wait for a new life starting
as a new day ahead half way around the world from there,

where there is another city we try on as if to wear it as our own,
its crown a glitz of light gem baubles blurred beneath a breath
of fog upon the bay. This is where we begin again.

And we, as if we might even know what we am doing here,
have come to rely on nothing but the dependable exchange
between the light and the dark, as we do each day, do each day.

81

# Note from a Motel

And here I am again, alone again, somewhere rainy
off an Interstate connection, bleary-eyed and weary,
hopscotching map lines figuring how to get back,
back to you. I've held on to the note you slipped me,
a ticket out, heavy-handed as a stone cutter's
epitaph in granite: *I've had it, it's too much,*
                                *this is where it all stops.*

And I know it's not the end of the world,
even in this loneliness the panic of *No Vacancy* signs
along the dark and rain soaked coast I've roamed.
But here, the quiet could be deadly.

Do you know what I mean? Can you possibly
get this? I could become some woman in a dim lit bar,
hiking up her skirt in an urgency for love. Could you
forgive that? Have you heard this before?

But things could be worse. I could bump around
outside up against the muggy midnight sky, weepy
for you. By the time this gets to you, there could be
a tidal wave, cars might crash, ships wreck, a star
burn out. And we will have had this accident
of time apart to sleep and dream and think.

Yet I do nothing but dread our days cut short.
You don't believe me? Here's the key.
Let your senses bring you to me. Drag your bags in
here across the floor. The earth might move.
We could really make some noise.

# WHILE I AM AWAY

While I am away, and you turn inside
the sheets to stretch and yawn, try
to remember other mornings. Waking up
to French Roast and toast beneath the thin
white veil of summer light. Shift opened
at a crossed leg. Talking news. Birds
a flurry of wings at the feeder. A span
of sand. Wind wild hair. The sprite of kites
climbing cloud flowered skies.

And since I must remind you
not to let our flush of sweet peas die
for water, leaves turn under, blossoms
tumble from the vine, I will remind you
of what I will bring back to you.
A bauble of crystal to spin new light.
My fingers making something new
from everything that was. There will be
plenty of time for this.

So when you turn inside the night covers,
reach for my hand, its ghost cupped
at the curve of your hip, never mind
those long cold shadows of regret.
Inside us there is room enough for stars
to sprawl a flawless slate of sky.
So that you will not forget me, come here now.
I want to whisper in your ear.
Lie still. My kiss is at your neck.

# Trilogy of Land, Sea, Sky

This land of blue-eyed grasses and wild iris flirting
the sunny bracken, its bumblebees in berry blossoms,
the little spittle bugs on the huckleberry, a nurse log
bearded in moss behind the wild azalea, all hanging on

while seaside supply ships tack and jibe the bay,
careen and beach where last night's breaker waves
tossed up drift logs, sea stars, crab shells, agates
beading the coast in mighty booms reverberating.

And I was there, too, beneath that boozy moon
hanging out all my sins on its beams, all a swagger
under the barrel-chested clouds, so starry-eyed
with the peachy sunset ribboning the horizon,

its incandescent streamer bearing some message
I stand here still straining to decipher.

# ON ANCIENT WINGS

The little black grackles keep coming back
   for more.
They pick stale caramel corn from the sack,
   swallow
them whole, toe-dancing snowdrifts, all bobs
   in the delight
of the find. Even city doves wait their turn
   in the blizzard
of birds, in the yes yes yes of it.

   One flies
a warning, yellow-eyed at my face, as if
   I would
rush her feathers for a spicy hat, her belly
   for a bit
of meat to glaze, breast a bone from which
   to pull a wish.
From where I stand behind the window glass,
   it is only this
upon which I fix my eyes and my desire—

   the wind
along lacy wing bars, early light that flirts
   a wash
across the crown, sheen on bellies and bobs.
   If these
blackbirds survive the cold another morning,
   then so will I.
We have these things that hold us here,
   this watch,
sweet feast, the voiceless scavenging—
   the yes oh yes of it.

# Revering a Hawk from a Mountaintop

(after Robert Bly's "Hunting Pheasants in a Cornfield")

**I**

What is so fetching here about a bird crossing sky?
It is a hawk, fire-tipped wings spread wide and strangely
Silent. My eyes drift with it at dusk in Autumn.
I crook my neck from this mound of earth and look.

**II**

It rained all day in skips along a bone-dry season.
The muddy trails are strewn with slips of leaves.
The sun is setting down, birds in branches atwitter.
A small happiness wends in where I stand and watch.

**III**

The mind delights in distances beyond what it can circle,
Endures alone inside stretches of still pastureland.
The moon tames the sky with patches of new quiet,
And I content myself with bird wings in my head.

**IV**

Day folds in its own wide wings, pulls up night covers,
I stay close to the ground and my own skin I crawl in.
I do not know all the things I could yet come to love.
At twilight, we do what we must, eyes turned upward.

# SOMETHING ABOUT THE POET:

Andrena Zawinski, an award winning writer and educator, was born and raised in Pittsburgh, PA and now lives and teaches writing in the San Francisco Bay Area. Her other collections include *Traveling in Reflected Light* (Pig Iron Press 1995), *Zawinski's Greatest Hits* (Pudding House 2002), and *Taking the Road Where It Leads* (Poets Corner Press 2008). Zawinski is Features Editor at Poetry Magazine.

# Acknowledgements:

The author gratefully acknowledges these publications in which work from this collection appeared, sometimes in earlier versions: *5AM, Alameda Island Anthology, Bay Area Poets Coalition Anthology, Bylines Literary Calendar, Cloud View Poets Anthology, Comstock Review, Copper Nickel, Crab Creek Review, California Quarterly, Eating Her Wedding Dress Anthology, Eclipse, Good News, Haight Ashbury Literary Journal, Heliotrope, Into the Teeth of the Wind, Karamu, Letters to the World Anthology, mm review, Many Mountains Moving, Monterey Poetry Review, Nimrod International Literary Journal, Not a Muse Anthology, Oakland's Neighborhoods Anthology, Only the Sea Keeps Anthology, Pacific Review, Paterson Literary Review, Pittsburgh Post Gazette, Potomac Review, Psychological Perspectives Journal of Jungian Thought, Quarterly West, Rattle, Raven Chronicles, Red Rock Review, Rive Gauche, Rockhurst Review, Runes Review, Santa Clara Review, San Francisco Reader, Slipstream, Sow's Ear, The Progressive Magazine, WordWrights, Xanadu.* The author is additionally grateful to the artistic organizations and online publications that reprinted or awarded many poems honors.

## Author's Notes:

Ekphrastic poetry in the second section is inspired by the following visual art, exhibitions, or books: "Against the Wind," wall engravings at Angel Island Immigration Station and Lim's book *Island*; "Altar Piece," Altares del Mundo Sacramento installation art; "Calendar Girl," calendar page, author unknown; "Dreamboat," Magritte's (1947) *Philosophy of the Boudoir*; "Ghosts in the Garden," The Round Church photo by the author; "I Have Seen Terezin," Friedl Bicker-Brandeis' painting "Untitled, 1944, Terezin" and the book *I Never Saw Another Butterfly: Children's Drawings and Poems from Terezin Concentration Camp*; "Impressions en Plein Air," Monet's (1899) *Water-Lily Pond*; "Something About," bird photos by the author; "The Largeness of Flowers," *A Poetry of Things* O'Keeffe exhibit, San Francisco Legion of Honor; "The Narrative Thread," quilt installation of *Contemporary Women's Embroidery in Rural India*, Washington D. C. National Museum of Women in the Arts.

(Italicized matter in "I Thought We Would Survive It All," is from Georgeann Rettberg's *Steelworker's Family* book.)